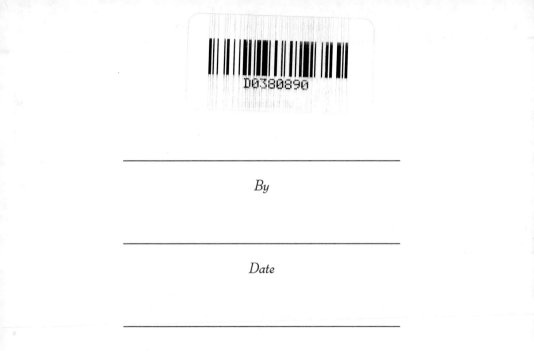

_____

_By_

_____

Date

_____

The
Quotable Christian

Favorite Quotes from Notable Christians

Compiled by Helen Hosier

BARBOUR
PUBLISHING, INC.
Uhrichsville, Ohio

© MCMXCVIII by Helen Hosier

ISBN 1-57748-173-9

Published by Barbour Publishing, Inc.
        P.O. Box 719
        Uhrichsville, Ohio 44683
        http://www.barbourbooks.com

 Member of the
Evangelical Christian
Publishers Association

Printed in the United States of America.

TABLE OF CONTENTS

Adversity arranges the assets of our balance sheet
in accordance with the perfect accountancy of heaven.

❧

Herbert Lockyer
Dark Threads the Weaver Needs

*G*od is not an arsonist; He is a refiner.

❧

Source unknown

*T*he greatest sermons I have ever heard
were not preached from pulpits, but from sickbeds.

❧

M. R. DeHaan
Broken Things

Affliction

*I*n the day of prosperity we have many refuges to resort to;
in the day of adversity, only One.

❧

Horatius Bonar

I believe in angels because the Bible says there are angels;
and I believe the Bible to be the true Word of God.

❧

Billy Graham
Angels: God's Secret Agents

T he function of God's angels is
to execute the plan of divine providence,
even in earthly things.

❧

Thomas Aquinas

*L*ord, bend that proud and stiffnecked I,
Help me to bow the head and die,
Beholding Him on Calvary
Who bowed His head and died for me.

❦

Roy Hession
The Calvary Road

*L*et the Bible fill the memory,
rule the heart and guide the feet.

❧

Henrietta Mears
431 Quotes

*D*ecisions which are made in the light of God's Word
are stable and show wisdom.

❧

Vonette Z. Bright
For Such a Time As This

*H*uman knowledge must be understood to be loved,
but divine knowledge must be loved to be understood.

❧

Pascal

I believe the Bible is the best gift God has ever given to men.
All the good from the Saviour of the world
is communicated to us through this book.

❧

Abraham Lincoln

*I*n teaching me the way of life,
the Bible has taught me the way to live;
it taught me how to die.

❧

Billy Sunday

Υou can judge how far you have risen
in the scale of life by asking one question:
How wisely and how deeply do I care?. . .
To be Christianized is to be sensitized:
Christians are people who care.

❧

E. Stanley Jones
A Song of Ascents

No man can use his Bible with power unless
he has the character of Jesus in his heart.

❧

Alan Redpath
The Making of a Man of God

Persons of true godly character are
neither optimists nor pessimists,
but realists who have confidence in God.

🌺

Warren W. Wiersbe
Why Us? When Bad Things Happen to God's People

God is willing to make the best of us,
but we have to be willing to give Him the worst of us.

❧

Helen Hosier
It Feels Good to Forgive

Spiritual freedom is
the state of having become childlike with God.
Not childish, childlike.
Jesus said that unless or until we become as little children
we could not possibly understand the kingdom of God.

❧

Eugenia Price
The Wider Place

*W*hen the clever are really intelligent,
they look to children for answers.
For our sake, Jesus became a vulnerable child.

❦

Diane M. Komp, M.D.
A Window to Heaven

*W*hen Jesus put the little child in the midst of His disciples,
He did not tell the little child to become like His disciples,
He told the disciples to become like the little child.

❦

Ruth Bell Graham
It's My Turn

I do not know how the Spirit of Christ performs it,
but He brings us choices through which we
never-endingly change, fresh and new, into His likeness.

✻

Joni Eareckson Tada
Choices & Changes

One of the greatest ways God changes me is
by bringing Scripture to mind I have hidden deep in my heart.
And He always picks the right Scripture at the right time.

❦

Evelyn Christenson
"Lord, Change Me!"

Choices and Changes

O God give me serenity to accept the things I cannot change,
courage to change the things I can,
and wisdom to know the difference.

❦

St. Francis of Assisi

I believe that Christ died for me because it is incredible;
I believe that He rose from the dead because it is impossible.

❧

One of the early church fathers

God is never in the self-improvement plan,
but always in the Christ-replacement plan. . . .

❦

Alan Redpath
Victorious Christian Faith

*T*he stops of a good man are ordered by
the Lord as well as his steps.

❧

George Müller

Christ is not valued at all unless He is valued above all.

St. Augustine

*T*he best way to get on your feet is on your knees.

❧

Source unknown

*S*atan may build a hedge about us and
fence us in and hinder our movements,
but he cannot roof us in and prevent our looking up.

❧

J. Hudson Taylor

*S*anta Claus never died for anybody.

❧

Craig Wilson

Christ's Birth

A baby's hands in Bethlehem
Were small and softly curled.
But held within their dimpled grasp
The hope of all the world.

❧

Leslie Savage

Christmas is His [Christ's] monogram,
stenciled on our hearts,
recalling to us year by year that
"no more is God a Stranger.". . . .

❦

Charles L. Allen and Charles L. Wallis
When Christmas Came to Bethlehem

The Word of God is the "antibiotic" that seeks out and destroys the viruses that would plague the life of the church.

❦

A. W. Tozer
Jesus, Author of Our Faith

*I*t is a true sign of the church when
true Christians love one another.
The church is to be a loving church in a dying culture.

❦

Francis Schaeffer
The Great Evangelical Disaster

The Church

As alien and archaic as the idea may seem,
the task of the church is not to make men and women happy;
it is to make them holy.

❧

Charles Colson
The Body

The church is not a gallery for
the exhibition of eminent Christians,
but a school for the education of imperfect ones.

❧

Henry Ward Beecher

Comfort

We are not placed on this earth
to see through each other,
but to see each other through.

❧

William M. Kinnaird
Joy Comes With the Morning

One of the more significant things
He [God] will bring out of our grief and depression is
an ability to walk constructively with others through theirs.
In fact, one of the purposes of God's comfort is to
equip us to comfort others.

❦

David B. Biebel
Jonathan, You Left Too Soon

*W*hen you are in the dark, listen,
and God will give you a very precious message
for someone else when you get into the light.

❧

Oswald Chambers

God does not comfort us to make us comfortable,
but to make us comforters.

❦

Dr. Jowett

*T*he stiff and wooden quality about our religious lives is
a result of our lack of holy desire.
Complacency is a deadly foe of all spiritual growth. . . .
He [God] waits to be wanted.

❧

A. W. Tozer
The Pursuit of God

*T*here is no pillow so soft as a clear conscience.

❧

French proverb

Conviction is worthless until it is converted into conduct.

❦

Thomas Carlyle

*D*ust, rusty nails, and blood notwithstanding,
the ground at the foot of the cross is
the only vantage point from which to view life clearly.
To see things there is to see them truly.

❧

Rebecca Manley Pippert
Hope Has Its Reasons

*T*he way of the Cross is
no nightmarish death march into oblivion,
with just one sacrifice piled on another.
It is a straight line to God.
It leads home.

❧

Sherwood Eliot Wirt
The Cross On the Mountain

Death is the golden key that opens the palace of eternity.

✿

John Milton

*L*ive in Christ, die in Christ,
and the flesh need not fear death.

❧

John Knox

Death marks the beginning, not the end.
It is our journey to God.

❧

Billy Graham
Hope for the Troubled Heart

A good starting point for dying well is to live well.

❧

Betty Carlson
Life Is for Living

*"H*e is no fool who gives
what he cannot keep to gain what he cannot lose."

❧

Jim Elliot, as quoted by Elisabeth Elliot
Shadow of the Almighty

*I*n life we decide our destiny at death.

❦

Joseph Bayly
A View From A Hearse, A Christian View of Death

*I*t is a delightful thing when you know that you are
close enough to the adversary that you can hear him roar!
Too many Christians never get into "lion country" at all!. . .
[the devil] is a dark and sinister foe
dedicated to the damnation of humans.

❧

A. W. Tozer
I Talk Back to the Devil

God does not dispense strength and encouragement
like a druggist fills your prescription.
The Lord doesn't promise to give us something to take
so we can handle our weary moments.
He promises us Himself. That is all.
And that is enough.

❦

Charles W. Swindoll
Encourage Me

*D*iscipleship means allegiance to the suffering Christ,
and it is therefore not at all surprising that
Christians should be called upon to suffer.

❧

Dietrich Bonhoeffer
The Cost of Discipleship

*I*f God were proud He would hardly have us. . .
but He is not proud,
He stoops to conquer.

✢

C. S. Lewis
The Problem of Pain

Never doubt in the dark what God told you in the light.

❦

V. Raymond Edman

*W*hat we are is more significant,
in the long run, than what we do.
It is impossible for a man to give what he does not have.

❧

Elton Trueblood
The New Man for Our Time

The choices of time are binding in eternity.

❦

Dr. Jack MacArthur

We who live in this nervous age would be wise to
meditate on our lives and our days long and
often before the face of God and on the edge of eternity.
For we are made for eternity as certainly as
we are made for time, and as
responsible moral beings we must deal with both.

❧

A. W. Tozer
The Knowledge of the Holy

*T*his short, earthly life,
important and significant though it may be in its setting,
is no more than a prelude
to a share in the timeless Life of God.

❧

J. B. Phillips
New Testament Christianity

*L*ive near to God,
and all things will appear little to you
in comparison with eternal realities.

❧

Robert Murray McCheyne

Those who live in the Lord
never see each other for the last time.

An old German motto

*T*he difference between catching men and catching fish is
that you catch fish that are alive, and they die;
you catch men that are dead and bring them to life. . . .

❧

Dawson Trotman, as quoted by Robert D. Foster
The Navigator

So many suffer so much
while so few sacrifice so little.

❧

Dr. Bob Pierce,
founder of World Vision

*E*xcellence is not perfection,
but essentially a desire to be strong in the Lord
and for the Lord.

❦

Cynthia Heald
Becoming a Woman of Excellence

Do we so appreciate the marvellous salvation
of Jesus Christ that we are our utmost for His highest?

❧

Oswald Chambers
My Utmost for His Highest

Excellence

With the goodness of God to desire our highest welfare,
the wisdom of God to plan it, what do we lack?
Surely we are the most favored of all creatures.

❧

A. W. Tozer
The Knowledge of the Holy

God is a specialist;
He is well able to work our failures into His plans. . . .
Often the doorway to success is entered
through the hallway of failure.

❦

Erwin W. Lutzer
Failure: The Back Door to Success

Little faith will bring your souls to Heaven,
but great faith will bring Heaven to your souls.

❧

Charles H. Spurgeon

*F*aith is two empty hands held open
to receive all of the Lord Jesus.

❧

Alan Redpath
Victorious Christian Faith

Faith is believing beyond the optic nerve.

❦

Author unknown

*F*aith is like radar which sees through the fog—
the reality of things at a distance
that the human eye cannot see.

❧

Corrie ten Boom
Tramp for the Lord

*F*aith is obedience at home and looking to the Master; obedience is faith going out to do His will.

❧

Andrew Murray
With Christ in the School of Prayer

*F*aith never knows where it is being led
or it would not be faith.
True faith is content to travel under sealed orders.

❧

J. Oswald Sanders
Spiritual Manpower

Faith is our spiritual oxygen.
It not only keeps us alive in God,
but enables us to grow stronger. . . .

❦

Joyce Landorf Heatherley
The Inheritance

When you enroll in the "school of faith,"
you never know what may happen next. . . .
The life of faith presents challenges that
keep you going—and keep you growing!

❦

Warren W. Wiersbe
Be Obedient

God didn't call us to be successful,
just faithful.

❧

Mother Teresa

*W*hen God forgives He forgets.
He buries our sins in the sea and
puts a sign on the bank saying,
"No Fishing Allowed."

❧

Corrie ten Boom
Tramp for the Lord

$\mathcal{M}$any people who ask for God's help are disappointed.
The reason?
They should begin by asking for God's forgiveness.

🐝

Erwin W. Lutzer
Failure: The Back Door to Success

*D*oing an injury puts you below your enemy;
revenging an injury makes you even with him;
forgiving an injury sets you above him!

❧

Source unknown

*F*orgiveness is not an emotion. . . .
Forgiveness is an act of the will,
and the will can function regardless of
the temperature of the heart.

❧

Corrie ten Boom
Tramp for the Lord

*T*here is only one place
we can put our guilt to find a true sense of forgiveness—
on the back of the crucified Christ.

❧

David Seamands
Putting Away Childish Things

*F*orgiveness is
the antiseptic for our emotional wounds.

❦

Floyd McClung, Jr.
The Father Heart of God

The best times in life are made a thousand times better
when shared with a dear friend.

❧

Luci Swindoll
You Bring the Confetti. . .God Brings the Joy

Oh the comfort,
the inexpressible comfort of feeling safe with a person;
having neither to weigh thoughts nor measure words but
to pour them all out, just as it is,
chaff and grain together,
knowing that a faithful hand will take and sift them,
keeping what is worth keeping, and then,
with the breath of kindness blow the rest away.

❦

Marian Evans (George Eliot)

Few of the valuable things in life "just happen."
When they happen it is because we recognize their importance
and devote ourselves to them. . . .
rule number one for deepening your friendships is:
Assign top priority to your relationships.

❧

Alan Loy McGinnis
The Friendship Factor

Friendship is one of the sweetest joys of life.
Many might have failed beneath the bitterness of
their trial had they not found a friend.

❦

Charles H. Spurgeon

T rue friends are people who care for one another
more "in spite of" than "because of."

❧

Betty Carlson
Life Is for Living

God needs no defenders.
He is the eternal Undefended.

❦

A. W. Tozer
The Knowledge of the Holy

*T*hou hast formed us for Thyself,
and our hearts are restless till they find rest in Thee.

❧

St. Augustine

*G*od's guidance is
even more important than common sense. . . .
I can declare that the deepest darkness is
outshone by the light of Jesus.

❦

Corrie ten Boom
Tramp for the Lord

*M*en give advice;
God gives guidance.

❧

Leonard Ravenhill

God had an only Son and
He made Him a missionary.

❧

David Livingstone

He who consciously or unconsciously has chosen
to ignore God is an orphan in the universe. . . .

❧

Emile Cailliet
Alone at High Noon

*T*he modern intelligent mind, . . .
has got to be shocked afresh by
the audacious central Fact—
that as a sober matter of history
God became One of us.

❦

J. B. Phillips
New Testament Christianity

*T*he world is perishing for lack of the knowledge of God
and the church is famishing for want of His presence.
The instant cure of most of our religious ills would be
to enter the Presence in spiritual experience,
to become suddenly aware that we are in God
and that God is in us.
This would. . .cause our hearts to be enlarged. . . .

❧

A. W. Tozer
The Pursuit of God

*I*n the absence of any other proof,
the thumb alone would convince me
of God's existence.

❦

Sir Isaac Newton

It is important to learn respect and obedience
to the "inner must" if godliness is
to be a state of soul with me.

❧

Jim Elliot, edited by Elisabeth Elliot
The Journals of Jim Elliot

*H*oliness means godliness and
godliness is rooted in God-centeredness.

❦

James Packer
Your Father Loves You

$\mathcal{W}$e ought not to try and be
more religious than God Himself.

❧

Dietrich Bonhoeffer

*I*n times of uncertainty, wait.
Always, if you have any doubt, wait.
Do not force yourself to any action.
If you have a restraint in your spirit,
wait until all is clear, and do not go against it.

❧

Mrs. Charles E. Cowman
Streams in the Desert

*T*he man who walks with God
always gets to his destination.

❦

Henrietta Mears
431 Quotes

A God wise enough to
create me and the world I live in is
wise enough to watch out for me.

❦

Philip Yancey
Where Is God When It Hurts?

God will prove to you
how good and acceptable and perfect His will is
when He's got His hands on the steering wheel of your life.

✵

Stuart & Jill Broscoe
Life, Liberty and the Pursuit of Holiness

Never be afraid to trust
an unknown future to a known God.

❦

Source unknown

*H*e who abandons himself to God
will never be abandoned by God!

❧

Source unknown

Υou can drive a better business at the mercy-seat
than in the world's jangling markets.
You will get more relief from the righteous Lord
than from ungodly men.

❧

Charles H. Spurgeon
Sermons (Preached in 1888), Vol. 19

Big problems?
God is bigger.

❧

Source unknown

*W*hen God is going to do a wonderful thing,
He begins with a difficulty.
When He is going to do a very wonderful thing,
He begins with an impossibility!

❦

Charles Inwood

Man's extremity is God's opportunity.

Matthew Henry

Grace is the good pleasure of God that inclines Him
to bestow benefits upon the undeserving.

❧

A. W. Tozer
The Knowledge of the Holy

Man is born broken. He lives by mending.
The grace of God is the glue.

❧

Eugene Field

*T*he will of God will never take you
where the grace of God cannot keep you.

🍀

Author unknown

Time heals grief;
love prevents scar tissue from forming.

❦

Joseph Bayly
A View From a Hearse, A Christian View of Death

Growing in any area of the Christian life takes time, and the key is daily sitting at the feet of Jesus.

❧

Cynthia Heald
Becoming a Woman of Excellence

I'm not all that I ought to be,
but I thank God I'm not what I used to be.
If I keep praying and asking God to make me to be what
He wants me to be, some day I will be what I need to be. . .
in my walk with the Lord,
I'm not saying I'm better than others—
I'm just better than I was.

❦

Frances Kelley
Better Than I Was

Heaven is
a prepared place for a prepared people.

❧

Source unknown

*H*uman history is
an outworking of his [God's] purpose:
history is his story.

❧

James Packer
Your Father Loves You

*T*here is no detour to holiness.
Jesus came to the resurrection through the cross,
not around it.

❧

Leighton Ford

*T*he Holy Spirit is the divine substitute on earth today
for the bodily presence of the Lord Jesus Christ
two thousand years ago.

❦

Alan Redpath
Victorious Christian Faith

*W*hether we preach, pray, write, do business, travel,
take care of children or administer the government—
whatever we do—
our whole life and influence should be filled
with the power of the Holy Spirit.

❧

Charles G. Finney

*T*he believing Christian has hope
as he stands at the grave of a loved one who is with the Lord,
for he knows that the separation is not forever.
It is a glorious truth that those who are in Christ
never see each other for the last time.

❧

Billy Graham
Hope for the Troubled Heart

*I*f we are to have hope amidst
all the menaces and threats of today's world,
it has got to be a sturdy and well-founded hope. . . .
It is essential that we recapture
and hold fast the New Testament idea that God is
the "God of hope" *Romans 15:13.* . . .
He is either a present help or He is not much help at all.

❧

J. B. Phillips
New Testament Christianity

*"H*ope thou in God" *Psalm 42:5.*
Oh, remember this:
There is never a time when we may not hope in God. Whatever
our necessities, however great our difficulties,
and though to all appearance help is impossible,
yet our business is to hope in God,
and it will be found that it is not in vain.

❦

George Müller

One of the best ways I know to infuse you with hope is
Romans 15:13: "May the God of hope fill you with
all JOY and peace as you trust in him,
so that you will overflow with HOPE."
And do you know what h-o-p-e stands for?
Hope Offers Peace Eternal!

❧

Barbara Johnson
I'm So Glad You Told Me What I Didn't Wanna Hear

Joy is
the characteristic by which God uses us
to re-make the distressing into the desired,
the discarded into the creative.
Joy is prayer—Joy is strength—Joy is love—
Joy is a net of love by which you can catch souls.

❦

Mother Teresa

*T*he surest mark of a Christian is not faith,
or even love, but joy.

❧

Samuel M. Shoemaker

*T*he joy that Jesus gives is
the result of our disposition being at one
with his own disposition.

❧

Oswald Chambers

When I think of God,
my heart is so full of joy that the notes leap and dance
as they leave my pen;
and since God has given me a cheerful heart,
I serve him with a cheerful spirit.

❧

Franz Joseph Haydn

We all go through pain and sorrow,
but the presence of God,
like a warm comforting blanket,
can shield us and protect us,
and allow the deep inner joy to surface,
even in the most devastating circumstances.
I know, because I have been there. . . .

❦

Barbara Johnson
Fresh Elastic for Stretched Out Moms

*J*oy is
the flag that's flying when the King is on the throne.

❧

Mary Crowley
A Pocketful of Hope

*J*oy can be the echo
of God's life within you.

❧

Duane Pederson
On Lonely Street with God

Kind words are the music of the world.

❧

Frederick William Faber

*W*hile great brilliance and intellect are to be admired,
they cannot dry one tear or mend a broken spirit.
Only kindness can accomplish this.

❧

John M. Drescher
Now Is the Time to Love

*T*he nicest thing we can do for our heavenly Father,
is to be kind to one of His children.

❦

St. Teresa of Avila

God is too wise to ever make a mistake
and too loving to ever be unkind. . . .

❧

Duane Pederson
On Lonely Street with God

'*T* was a thief said the last
kind word to Christ:
Christ took the kindness
and forgave the thief.

❧

Robert Browning

Υou can't speak a kind word too soon,
for you never know how soon it will be too late.

🍂

Our Daily Bread

Life's major pursuit is not knowing self. . .
but knowing God. . . .
Unless God is the major pursuit of our lives,
all other pursuits are dead-end streets,
including trying to know ourselves.

❧

Charles R. Swindoll
Growing Deep in the Christian Life

*P*art of what it means to be God's children is
to accept that He knows,
and that He will bring what is best into our lives—
not what we want every time,
but what is ultimately best for us.

❧

Charles Paul Conn
Father Care: What It Means to Be God's Child

*L*et laughter reign when it comes.
It is oil for the engines that rise to
challenges and work miracles.

❧

Donald E. Demaray
Laughter, Joy and Healing

*L*aughter dulls the sharpest pain
and flattens out the greatest stress.
To share it is to give a gift of health. . . .

❦

Barbara Johnson
I'm So Glad You Told Me What I Didn't Wanna Hear

Christ is the only liberator
whose liberation lasts forever.

❧

Malcolm Muggeridge
Jesus Rediscovered

Man is lonely mainly because
he has been disconnected from the divine presence. . . .

❧

James Johnson
Loneliness Is Not Forever

*L*oneliness is the first thing which
God's eye named as not good.

❧

John Milton

*L*ife with Christ is endless love;
without Him it is a loveless end.

❧

Billy Graham
Hope for the Troubled Heart

*R*iches take wings,
comforts vanish, hope withers away,
but love stays with us.
God is love.

❧

Lew Wallace
author of *Ben Hur*

*L*ove accepts the trying things of life
without asking for explanations.
It trusts and is at rest.

❧

Amy Carmichael
Edges of His Ways

*E*very circumstance in life,
no matter how crooked and distorted
and ugly it appears to be,
if it is reacted to in love and forgiveness and obedience,
[God's] will can be transformed.

❧

Hannah Hurnard
Hinds' Feet on High Places

Brotherly love
is still the distinguishing badge
of every true Christian.

✿

Matthew Henry
Moments of Meditation

We are not made for law,
but for love.

❧

George Macdonald

 Υou always win a better response with love.

❦

Helen Hosier
You Never Stop Being a Parent

*I*t's no secret.
The ministry of the church is a genuine concern for others.
We need to stop talking about it and start doing it.
Rise and shine, friend.
Everyone you meet today is
on heaven's Most Wanted list.

❧

Charles R. Swindoll
Rise & Shine: A Wake-up Call

*T*he only real mistake is one from which we learn nothing,
and I think I have learned much. . . .
[But] I think we must be patient with ourselves,
just as God is infinitely patient with us.

❧

John Powell
He Touched Me: My Pilgrimage of Prayer

God's mark is
on everything that obeys Him.

❦

Martin Luther

A life of obedience is
not a life of following a list of do's and don'ts,
but it is allowing God to be original in our lives.

❦

Vonette Z. Bright
For Such a Time As This

*G*od whispers to us in our pleasures,
speaks in our conscience,
but shouts in our pains:
it is His megaphone to rouse a deaf world.

❧

C. S. Lewis
The Problem of Pain

Simply put, our suffering is temporary—
just like the bodies in which we are suffering are temporary.
But the rewards we are accumulating while in
these temporary bodies are eternal. . . .
God has allowed us to participate in a system by
which the temporal can be used to gain what is eternal.

❧

Charles Stanley
How to Handle Adversity

Pain

Jesus' death is the cornerstone of the Christian faith. . . .
Jesus in a sense dignified pain.
Of all the kinds of lives he could have lived,
he chose a suffering one. . . .
Christ did not stay on the cross.

❧

Philip Yancey
Open Windows

*F*or whatever reason God chose to make man as he is—
limited and suffering and subject to sorrows and death—
He had the honesty and courage to
take His own medicine.

❧

Dorothy Sayers

*R*esolutely
slam and lock the door on past sin and failure,
and throw away the key!

❦

J. Oswald Sanders
Lonely But Never Alone

*T*he better you become acquainted with God,
the less tensions you feel and the more peace you possess.

❦

Charles L. Allen
All Things Are Possible Through Prayer

*T*rue peace is not the absence of war
but the presence of God.

�֍

Our Daily Bread

Peace is full confidence that God is
Who He says He is
and that He will keep every promise in His Word.

❧

Dorothy Harrison Pentecost
My Pursuit of Peace

*R*epeating a prayer
does not bring peace with God.
But heartfelt faith in Christ does.

❧

Dr. Jack Van Impe
Israel's Final Holocaust

We can love Jesus in the hungry,
the naked, and the destitute who are dying. . . .
If you love, you will be willing to serve.
And you will find Jesus in
the distressing disguise of the poor.

❧

Mother Teresa
One Heart Full of Love

God is sparing in His eulogies
and entirely truthful in His statements.
He never scales down His standards
to meet our human frailty,
but rather empowers us to rise to them.

❧

J. Oswald Sanders
Spiritual Manpower

Υou must always work at practicing God's presence.
Not to advance in the spiritual life is to go backward. . . .
We should establish ourselves in a sense of God's presence
by continually conversing with Him.

❧

Brother Lawrence
The Practice of the Presence of God

*I*f we do not radiate the light of Christ around us,
the sense of the darkness
that prevails in the world will increase.

❦

Mother Teresa
One Heart Full of Love

*T*here is nothing more important in any life
than the constantly enjoyed presence of the Lord.
There is nothing more vital,
for without it we shall make mistakes,
and without it we shall be defeated.

❧

Alan Redpath
The Making of a Man of God

*W*hen we pray,
it is far more important to pray with a sense of
the greatness of God than with a sense of
the greatness of the problem.

❧

Evangeline Blood, Wycliffe Bible translator

Trouble and perplexity drive us to prayer,
and prayer driveth away trouble and perplexity.

❧

Melancthon

A demanding spirit,
with self-will as its rudder, blocks prayer. . . .
Prayer is men cooperating with God in
bringing from heaven to earth
His wondrously good plans for us.

❧

Catherine Marshall
Adventures in Prayer

Prayer is the link that connects us with God.
This is the bridge that spans every gulf and bears us
over every abyss of danger or of need.

❧

A. B. Simpson

God can hear the language of our worry
just as clearly as He hears the wailing of our words.
And He has promised that He will give us
a garment of praise for the spirit of heaviness.
(See Isaiah 61:3, KJV)

❦

Jill Briscoe
Fight For The Family

Men may spurn our appeals,
reject our message, oppose our arguments,
despise our persons—
but they are helpless against our prayers.

❧

J. Sidlow Baxter

God will do nothing
but in answer to prayer.

❧

John Wesley

God shapes the world by prayer.
The more praying there is in the world
the better the world will be,
the mightier the forces against evil.

❦

E. M. Bounds

*P*rayer is not a vending machine
which spits out the appropriate reward.
It is a call to a loving God to relate to us.

❦

Philip Yancy & Tim Stafford
Unhappy Secrets of the Christian Life

Life is fragile;
handle it with prayer.

❦

Source unknown

*W*hen I am dealing with an all-powerful,
all-knowing God, I, as a mere mortal,
must offer my petitions not only with persistence
but also with patience.
Someday I'll know why.

❦

Ruth Bell Graham
Prodigals and Those Who Love Them

Groanings which cannot be uttered are often prayers which cannot be refused.

❧

Charles H. Spurgeon

Problems

*W*hen life hands you problems,
put your problems in God's hands.

❧

Our Daily Bread

Salvation is not turning over a new leaf
but receiving a new life.

❧

Our Daily Bread

A recovery of the old sense of sin is essential to Christianity.

❦

C. S. Lewis
The Problem of Pain

Sin is in the world.
And sin is "missing the mark,"
missing God's perfect plan.
There is so much of this missing the mark that
it is going to impinge on
every person's life at some points.

❧

Catherine Marshall
Something More

*T*he committed man of God is against sin,
and all the powers of evil are against him.
In such a warfare there is no intermission at all.
The devil never takes five minutes' vacation!

❧

Alan Redpath
The Making of a Man of God

I am deeply a part of the problem
for which Christ died.

❧

Keith Miller
The Taste of New Wine

Sin won't keep you from heaven
but rejecting the pardon will.

❦

Iona Lyster

Look upon all sin as that which crucified the Saviour,
and see that it is exceeding sinful!

🦋

Charles H. Spurgeon

Suffering is
the badge of true discipleship. . . .

❧

Dietrich Bonhoeffer
The Cost of Discipleship

*T*he Bible is a Christian's guidebook,
and I believe the knowledge it sheds on pain and suffering is
the great antidote to fear for suffering people.
Knowledge can dissolve fear
as light destroys darkness.

❧

Philip Yancey
Where Is God When It Hurts?

*T*here is a time appointed for weakness and sickness,
when we shall have to glorify God by suffering,
and not by earnest activity. . . .
The path of trouble is the way home.
Lord, make this thought a pillow for many a weary head!

❧

Charles H. Spurgeon
Daily Help

It is doubtful whether God can bless a man greatly
until He has hurt him deeply.

❦

A. W. Tozer
The Root of the Righteous

*L*et us live and die with God:
sufferings will be ever sweet and pleasant to us,
while we abide with Him; and without Him,
the greatest pleasures will be but cruel anguish.

❧

Brother Lawrence
The Practice of the Presence of God

Human nature seems to need suffering to fit it for being a blessing to the world.

❧

Author unknown

*F*ill up the hours with what will last;
Buy up the moments as they go.
The life above, when this is past,
Is the ripe fruit of life below.

❧

Horatius Bonar

*T*here's something unique about having
only God to lean on in times of trial.

❧

Philip Yancey
Where Is God When It Hurts?

We must trust God.
We must trust not only that he does what is best,
but that he knows what is ahead.

❦

Max Lucado
A Gentle Thunder

*F*riend,
you can trust the Man that died for you.

❧

James McConkey

We have heard of many people
who trusted God too little,
but have you ever heard of anyone
who trusted Him too much?

❦

J. Hudson Taylor

Any wife who wants to can be trustworthy.
It isn't a matter of talent or intelligence;
it is a matter of integrity—
of being true to your word and getting the job done.

❦

Jeanne Hendricks
Afternoon: For Women At The Heart Of Life

*W*orship and worry cannot live in the same heart:
they are mutually exclusive.

❧

Ruth Bell Graham
Prodigals and Those Who Love Them